Writing and Self Publishing Christian Non Fiction

Simple Tips to Streamline Your First Book!

Matthew Robert Payne

Matthew can be contacted at http://www.matthewrobertpayneministies.net Donations to Matthew's ministry can be made at http://personal-prophecy-today.com

Cover Design: Maria Quiocho

Editing: Melanie Cardano

Back Cover Blurb: Melanie Cardano

The opinions expressed by the author are not necessarily those of Revival Waves of Glory Books & Publishing.

Revival Waves of Glory Books & Publishing
PO Box 596
Litchfield, IL 62056
United States of America
www.revivalwavesofgloryministries.com

Revival Waves of Glory Books & Publishing is committed to excellence in the publishing industry.

Published in the United States of America

Ebook: 978-3-9592-6494-5
Paperback: 978-0692496251
Hardcover: 978-1-943845-72-9

Dedications

June Payne- my mother

My mother is my greatest supporter and encourager. She has sowed ample amounts of time, money and love into my life. We speak nearly every day on the phone and a couple of times a year I spend a few weeks with her and my father Bob Payne on holidays. She is the sweetest and most supportive mother a person could have.

The writers I enjoyed

I have to thank all the writers that have written all the books I have read from cover to cover. I think a person has to have a passion for reading to be a good writer. I dedicate this book to all the writers that added to my life.

To You

I have taken the time to record the videos, had them transcribed, and the manuscript edited just for you. It is my prayer that you do more than read this book, but that you use it to help write and publish your first book. I would love to be sent a copy of your book sometime.

Acknowledgements

Maria Nordstokke.

I thank the typist that typed up the videos that made this book. Maria decided years ago to dedicate her time that she spends typing my videos to the Lord and she does not charge me for her typing. She does a wonderful job and I am so thankful for her. Maria can be hired at Upwork.com

Maria Quiocho.

I want to thank Maria for another cover I am happy with. She is a very busy lady and I am so pleased she has kept me as a client over the years and does her work for me. Maria can be hired at Upwork.com

Melanie Cardano.

I want to thank Melanie for her work copy editing this book. She did a great job, in little time, with lots of love. I want to thank her also for writing the back cover blurb for me. She is one of my greatest supporters. Melanie can by hired from Upwork.com

Bill Vincent.

I want to thank Bill of Revival Waves of Glory Books and Publishing for helping me self publish this book.

Bryn Phillips.

I want to thank Bryn for her donation to my ministry that allowed me to have the money required to publish with Bill.

Holy Spirit.

I want to thank you for giving me the inspiration for this book, the words to say, and the perseverance to get the job done.

Jesus Christ.

Thank you for being my closest friend. You have always loved me and always shown me that You love me. I am so thankful that you are a big part of my life.

My Readers.

Thank you for existing and giving me a desire to write.

Table of Contents

Introduction.

So now you are getting serious about writing your first book. I want to thank you first of all for doing something about it and buying my simple book. I want to warn you that I am not an expert writer and I am not highly educated. I am just a simple man that has written about ten books so far and as of publishing this one, I will have self published eight books.

Not all your answers are in here. Not every question you will have will be covered in this book, but this is a little book covering some of what I believe to be essentials if you are ever going to have success with your own books.

When you finally see your book on Amazon, you will be so proud and when money starts to come in you'll be happier. If you ever make your book free on the Kindle select program you might get really excited as you see hundreds of your books downloaded.

As you seek people to do reviews for your book, you will be surprised by some of the great thing they say about your book. When bad reviews come in you may get sad like me. But even Jesus with all His wisdom was mocked.

The craft of writing and self publishing a book is not an easy one, but it is highly rewarding and worthwhile. When you have written as many books as me, you may start to see people genuinely astonished when you tell them you are a writer and you have eight published books!

Read this book, refer back to it, and publish your book and write to me when it is done!

SECTION 1
First things First

1. What do you want to say?

Think of a very clear idea of what you want to say before you write a book. The success or failure of this will reflect on your book sales. If people find your idea clear as crystal the moment they open your book, then chances are that's already a sale. On the other hand, if your idea isn't clear and ultimately confuses people, then your mediocre sales will reflect that.

The first book that I wrote was a collection of articles called "The Musings of a Mad Prophet." Looking back, I realize that it's not essentially a good title. In the book, I talked about what it's like to have a bipolar condition. Despite my good intentions, I realized that the title was not captivating and the book didn't have a clear theme. It also suffered from having a mediocre cover that could have been better. Taking all those factors into consideration, it probably shouldn't come as a surprise that I manage to sell not more than 20 copies in 8 years. It's a far cry compared to now, where I have a book that sells 20 copies every month. Still, that experience taught me that having a clear idea and knowing how to talk about that idea has a lot of influence on whether you sell or not.

My second book was called "The Parables of Jesus Made Simple." Now, compared to my first book, I wrote this one out of the desire to explain the parables of Jesus through a modern context. I wrote it in a simplistic manner because other books that shared the same subject felt too theological, too hard to read and too hard to get into. So I sat down and recorded 54 videos of what I thought the parables were saying. Then, I had them transcribed and edited, and once that was done, I had it published. I am pleased to say that it fared better than my first book since it had managed to touch people and make them feel blessed upon reading it. For years, I had searched for the understanding of the parables. I scoured and read books about them, but I realized that they didn't provide the answers I sought. However, when I decided to write a book about it, I felt as if the Holy Spirit finally gave me an insight into what they meant. The book has a lot of good revelations in it. I still like to read it from time to time.

The next book that I consider a success is called "The Prophetic Supernatural Experience." The book is about the inner workings of a prophet's ministry office and what it looks like. It also provides insight to the three gifts of prophecy and how they operate in a person's life. For many years, I've been called to be a prophet of God and I've read book after book, trying to learn what my role as a prophet was. I asked myself questions like, what does a prophet do? How do they feel? How do they get trained? What do they do when they're in an office of a prophet? What does that look like? How do you understand it? I went through many years of reading books and listening to people, listening to videos, putting together an idea of what being a prophet actually means. When I came to the idea of writing a book, I did a series of videos. I first sat down with a piece of paper and wrote 55 chapter titles. One after another, I explained in those chapters what the gift of prophecy was, what the life of a prophet is and what one can expect in being a prophet. So what am I trying to say? I wanted to explain to people what it's like to be a prophet of the modern world and what it's like to operate with the gifts of prophecy. But I also wanted to bring a message that's prophetic, up to date and relevant that can change people's hearts and change the direction of the church. I picked another prophet to co-write the book with me, and ever since the book has been published, many people have written to me and thanked me for what we had written. Once again, I had written another book with a clear objective and through the feedback of the people who have read it, I achieved that purpose. This is the reason why it is important that you decide what you want to say.

I wrote a book titled "Your Identify in Christ." The book, which was 19 chapters long, talked about the different aspects of a person's identity as a follower of Christ. The 19 characteristics of our identity in Christ were taken from a Facebook post where someone described them, which was backed up by Scripture references next to each of the topics. I took that list and wrote a book on that using the Scripture references that were quoted. I didn't know the name of the person who posted the original post so I could not thank them. I wrote a whole book about it and I learned a lot about my identity, and until now, I'm still gleaning revelations from that book. There are cases where you'll find that you are compelled to write a book not only because it has to be written to inform your readers, but it has to be written to teach you something as well. I have read "Your Identity in Christ" for four times now, yet I still have to read it more to get the truths found in that book into me. The process of writing a book can be an enjoyable experience, you can learn a lot about yourself and about your subject matter as you put it on paper. As I read the books I have written, I am still surprised with the knowledge I shared in them. This can happen to you as well. You'll be surprised at how much information you can glean from the hidden parts of your brain.

First, you have to decide what you want to say. Do you have a wake up message for America? Do you have a message for people to come out of the Old Testament Law, or a message for the church to wake themselves up and face the new day? Do you have a message that will bring the Kingdom of God into the everyday streets of their cities? Do you want to do a call of repentance for the Nation of America or the nation that you're in? Do you want to bring insights and revelations from God to the contemporary

Christian world where you live? What's your message? What do you want to say? What is it that God has placed on your heart? More often, you will need to have a message that is going to take you more than 50 pages, a message that will carry through. Later in the book, I'll talk about how you need to have a message that will have "legs," one that will carry through the course of writing the whole book. Will your message sustain 50 pages or more? Is it a good message? As a writer, you may have written an article or two or a blog post before, or you may have done a regular post on Facebook and you've come across this decision that you want to write. If you've made that decision, then the first thing that you have to ask yourself is, "what do you want to write about?" What do you want to say? This is a very important thing to consider, the first step in finding the subject that you want to write about.

2. Who is your audience?

Who is your audience? In my book called "Prophetic Evangelism Made Simple," I talk about having the ability to walk up to strangers in the middle of the street and say, "Excuse me, I have this gift that, from time to time, allows me to give a message to a specific person. And today, I have message for you." They look at me, let me continue and then I deliver a message from God specifically for them. The message is not that Jesus wants you to repent, or that Jesus died for your sins and wants you to live for him like what most evangelists share. I may say something like, "You're a very honest person, a very caring person and you think really deeply. When you think about things, you really think deeply and you want to bring change in your life and bring change in other people's lives. God is going to use you in that ability to bring change and He's going to open up doors in the coming years where you can be promoted into a certain position and you can bring change into the world that you live in. So just press on. Keep being honest and being sincere and look out for that promotion. Look out for that opportunity where you'll be given more authority to bring change to your environment." They'll say, "Thank you" and I'll say, "God bless. I'm a Christian who has the gift of prophecy and that message was from God."

So that's the whole book on having the personality and understanding to reach out to people who are strangers on the streets of your city. It teaches you to be able to touch people with the gift of prophecy, to plant seeds in people's lives, seeds that God will find later and water through other people. That's "Prophetic Evangelism Made Simple." The subtitle, "Prophetic Seed Sowing" essentially means giving people messages that lead them one step towards their salvation. That book is not for everyone. It's intended for people who have a desire to reach other people with God's love through witnessing. You can guess that more people want to read about the parables than to read about how to witness to people through prophecy.

I've had my books at different prices in the past. I've had it at $0.99 and a lot more figures selling per month because I want to make it cheaper. But then, someone said to me, "Will someone really regard a 99 cent book with much respect? Will they really respect a 99 cent book or will they think it has cheap information contained in a cheap book? Better to price your book at $4.99 and have people pay real money for it and they'll respect and read it and you'll have more authority in a person's life." I made that change and the numbers of my book sales went down.

Who is your audience? Do you want to reach out to lost sheep? Do you want to write a book that will encourage people who are far away from the faith or slipped from their faith or living their lives in sin? Do you want to bring them back into repentance, bring them back into the fold with a loving message of grace from God or Jesus saying, "Come back, I love you"? Do you have a message for people who are stuck in religion? Do you have a message for those who read the Bible an hour each day, who pray for an hour each day, who tithe and go to church for one, maybe two times a week? Do you have a message of love for those bound up with rules and religion? Do you have a message for them to say, "Lighten up, God loves you. And here are all the reasons why God loves you and accepts you. You don't have to do anything to please Him." Do you have a message? Who do you want to reach?

This is very important. The title of the book is important as well and the reasons will be addressed in other areas of this book. The chapter titles addressing certain areas of the theme of the book also plays another important role, but you want to know essentially who your audience is. Who do you want to reach with what you have to say? Do you want to reach passionate Christians to equip them with tools on how to evangelize people in the streets? Do you want people to understand the parables of Jesus? To have them practically apply those parables in their day to day life? Do you want to essentially discipline Christians to have a more passionate and more obedient way of living for Jesus?

Do you want to reach people who are broken and have lived lives of sin? Do you want to reach them with an inspiring story of your life? Do you want to talk about how you struggled with so much sin, but eventually found respite in your intimate and beautiful relationship with Jesus Christ? Do you want to give broken people hope, understanding and love for Jesus Christ and a hope for a better tomorrow?

Do you want to reach people who want to write a book and have been contemplating writing one? That is the main purpose of this book. You need to have your audience in mind when you write a book. It helps you focus as you're writing the words, to have your audience in mind.

For instance, I wrote a book that's getting edited at the moment. It's called "Coping with your Pain and Suffering" and it was written essentially for two people that I know who are suffering from illness at the moment and haven't been cured by people's prayers. One woman has been in depression for about 10 years and can't feel the presence of God and she's in a really bad way. Another person I know is in a wheelchair for over 8 years and suffering tremendous pain. As I wrote this book, I have these two women in mind. I wanted to bring tears into their eyes, to make them understand that God loves them despite the fact that they're not healed nor well. It was essentially an apology to people who have had faith healers preach to them, who tried to heal them, but gave up on them, saying that they lack faith. That book was an encouragement and apology to those people on behalf of the Christian healers who have damaged them with their words. I wrote it out of the pain in my own life due to a mental illness. It was cathartic in a way.

As I was saying, you have to know what you want to say and know your audience. There are many people out there who consume books every single day of the week. I would say most of the people who read my books are Christians, but I know I write in such a simple way that even a person who is not a Christian would be blessed by them. Who do you want to read your book? Married women with a strong faith, young teens just setting out on their faith journey, or someone who has been hurt emotionally? What is your book about and who is going to read it?

3. What effect do you want your book to have?

What effect do you want your book to have? I have read a book on giving, *"Financial Stewardship"* by Andrew Wommack. In the book, it essentially confirmed that my approaches to tithing and giving to God were correct. It was a real encouragement to me and really inspired and encouraged me to live a giving sort of lifestyle. What effect do you want to have on people? Do you want to affect people in such a way that they go from giving only 1% of their income to 10%? Do you want to write a simple and accessible book with solid foundations on the practice, the rewards and the faith filled life that you can live through a life of giving? *"Financial Stewardship"* would be a good book for people who want to learn about the proper and balanced view on giving rather than what prosperity preachers preach.

One of the stories in *"Financial Stewardship"* told about Andrew's time in a pastor's church. In his meeting with the church's pastor, the latter said that the Holy Spirit had told him that his church was to pledge $50,000 to Andrew's ministry. However, the pastor told Andrew that he had no plan on how to do that. Andrew said, "I have an idea. I'll just ask the people who'll pray to God to grant them a thousand dollars in the next week to pledge to my ministry. I would ask who wants to pledge $1,000 and be prayed for that the Lord would provide."

And so Andrew went out and did that. He asked people who wanted prayer to stand on their feet and 50 people answered. Not 49, not 52, but exactly 50 people stood up. In the course of that week, money started pouring in to those 50 people. Some people got $1,000, some got $2,000 and some got $3,000 in money that came in for them supernaturally. There was such an excitement in the church that all those people were getting blessed with $1,000; other people who weren't in that first 50 started to pledge $1,000 in the hopes of making a profit off God. Every one of the people that pledged their $1,000 on the night that Andrew prayed got $1,000 off the Lord and was able to give Andrew $1,000. Every one of the people who pledged $1,000 after that night didn't get $1,000 off God. They just had to essentially give Andrew $1,000, but God didn't reward them. Andrew's point in that book was that God sees your heart. And He will bless and reward those who give to others, so long as they do not have a selfish motive in doing so.

That story really touched me. It was worth buying the book just for that message. Do you want to have that effect on people? It had a tremendous effect on me, on my heart. And I know that when I've given to ministries, the Lord sees my heart and knows that I'm blessed. I don't give so that I can get something in return. I give because I want to bless certain people. And because of that, I have a great relationship with giving.

"Destined to Reign" by Joseph Prince is a tremendous book on grace and how to remove condemnation from your life. It's a book that I've read twice and that I want to read again because I really need to get it into my spirit and understand. It has a very liberating message about grace and how we're loved and accepted: No matter what we do, we're loved and accepted without having to do anything for God. That had an amazing effect and left a really warm and positive glow in my heart when I think of that book. I've often shared in videos about *"Destined to Reign"* and how

magnificent it was. I wish I could buy a copy of that book for everyone reading this book and say, "Bless you."

What effect do you want to have on the person's heart? *"Financial Stewardship"* confirmed to me that I give for the right reasons and I'm a good giver. *"Destined to Reign"* showed me a new way of grace and a new understanding of the grace of God. God used Andrew Wommack and Joseph Prince to teach me all about grace and it was like I've been born a new man. I felt so good when I fully understood the grace of God. Where once I believed in an angry and vengeful God, now I believe in a loving God like Jesus. Both Andrew Wommack and Joseph Prince had a very big effect on me and they really were a watershed in my life. So again, how do you want to affect your audience? How do you want to affect the people reading your book? Do you want them to read "The Parables of Jesus" and remember what you wrote about them?

People who have read my book, "The Parables of Jesus Made Simple" and have taken what I said to heart are different people today. You too could change the way people think about others. Do you want people who walk down the street and see a homeless person to suddenly see themselves as the Good Samaritan? Do you want those people to walk up and offer the homeless change, buy them food or buy them a drink? Do you want to affect the person in such a way that when they see someone hungry, they give them something to eat like what the Sheep and the Goats parable suggests? That when they see someone thirsty, they give them a drink? That when they see a person lacking clothes, they help them buy clothes? That when they see them homeless, they take them in and give them a good meal? Do you want to affect change in people and make them a radical Christian, a passionate Christian that is a real disciple of Jesus Christ? What do you want to do? What affect do you want to have on people? This is something that you have to consider when you work out what book you want to write. This all plays into what you want to say, your audience and what effect you want to have on them.

4. Do you like to write?

This is a question you should be asking yourself before you attempt to write a book: How do you feel about writing? I'm not asking whether you passed with 80% or 90% in English at school. I'm not asking if you got tremendous marks for your essays at school. I'm not asking if you think you're a good writer. I'm saying if you like to write. Do you enjoy the process of thinking and putting your words down on paper? Do you enjoy the process of thinking, and creating sentence after sentence? Do you like to construct your words and formulate it in such a way that it makes an impact on people's lives?

There is a lot of typing between a chapter title and two pages of writing that makes sense. There is a lot to consider when you are making an argument for your readers. It will be a lot of work if you don't like writing. There is a lot to consider when you are going to write a book. Even after you have read this short book, you will still have blank pages to fill up. So if you're going to take on 50, 80 or 150 pages, you're going to have a lot more fun if you enjoy writing. Are you up to it?

There is real joy that can be found in creating something that is going to help other people. I had different things being said on the video portion of this part of the book. Today, as I read it, I deleted and rewrote it to be more suitable. This is something that you must be able to do. As a writer, you need to have the ability and the stomach to rewrite whole portions of your work. You can only take the time to do that if you enjoy writing, enjoy the process and you love your reader more than your own laziness (that is, if you have any like I do).

I personally find that writing is like having a conversation with someone. I find that as I sit down to type, it's as if you, the reader, is sitting down and listening to me. I carefully start to type and make my points one after another. Some people have written in their reviews of my books that my writing sounded like they were at a cafe having a conversation with me. That is the effect that I would like to have on people. I want people to be relaxed and comfortable. Do you like to make people comfortable with your writing?

5. Do you like to read?

I have heard people say before, "Writers are readers." There's a quote that says many writers are substantial readers. They read substantial amounts of books. I'm a person who reads a lot of books and enjoys them. To tell you the truth however, I really only finish about a quarter of the books I attempt to read. I can't tell from the blurb and the reviews about a book that it will be a page-turner unless someone actually writes and makes it a page-turner. I've read the whole Twilight series and some of those books were 600 pages or so, but I'm quite able to read such lengthy books and enjoy it. If a book compels me to read, I'll read a lot.

I enjoy reading fiction and non-fiction. I enjoy Christian and non-Christian books as well. As a writer, as a person who's going to write books, it would be helpful if you liked to read. This teaches you what a compelling story is. It shows you how to engage a person and how to keep their attention. It shows you how to develop a story and an argument. Through reading books, you'll realize how to make chapters, how to build on chapter after chapter and make a case with your book. There could be successful writers who aren't readers, but often, you'll find reviews written by writers of other books. You'll see a book advertised and you'll see a review, a short line written by Stephen King, who is Amazon's highest seller of books. If Stephen King writes, *"This is a riveting read by a great new author,"* it's a bit of a salesmanship we could all do with. Seeing endorsements by Stephen King means that even as Amazon's most popular writer, Stephen still reads other people's books.

If you like to read, then you're already half way in becoming a writer. You've understood the process of writing. You've understood what makes a good book. You want to make your book one that people don't put down, but it really depends on the person and what's being said in the book. I have some books by some tremendous authors. I just haven't finished reading them. It's not that I didn't spend money on them, it's just that those books didn't compel me to keep on reading.

Some people who pick up your book may start reading it, but will not finish it and that's a sad thing to contemplate. But there's also joy in knowing that there are certain people who'll pick up and finish your book and really enjoy it. If you like to read, that's a good thing and the more you read, the better it is. It's also helpful to read other people's books and write reviews on Amazon because as you do this, you can actually say "Matthew Robert Payne," author of "The Parables of Jesus Made Simple," and put a product link in the Amazon page. By doing this, you're highlighting the product so that people can press on the link and go to your book. I have over 100 reviews on Amazon and I advertise the most relevant book that I've written to that audience at the bottom of my reviews. I'm sure I sell a few books based on people reading one of my reviews. Of course, if you write a good review, people will know that you're an interesting writer. It's really helpful, once you've written a book, to continue reading books and writing reviews in Amazon and advertising the fact that you're an author.

6. Do you have supportive friends?

One thing that is fairly important when you're endeavouring to do a new project or launch off into a new career as a writer is having friends around you who are supportive. Friends are people who believe in your future, who accept your past, and love you just the way you are. I have a pastor in my church who is really loving and supportive and he loves to hear what books I'm writing, what process I'm up to and we spend time talking about it each week in his office. He loves to hear what I'm doing and he loves to encourage me in what I'm doing. I've also got friends on Facebook who are supportive.

When you're going to make a change, when you're going to say something that'd going to disturb Satan's kingdom, when you're going to write something that's going to bring forth fruit in people's lives and encourage people, Satan's not going to be happy about it. He'll try and discourage you through the whole act of writing. And even after you've published your book, you may still be attacked. I certainly can testify to getting attacked with depression for 2 or 3 weeks every time I've published a book simply because I've disturbed Satan's kingdom. When you are under attack, it is helpful to have friends to support you.

When you're in the middle of doubting yourself while going through the process of writing a book, it's good to have friends who can read parts of your book and be supportive and hold you up. It's good to have people who love you before you've written your book and people who will love you even more once they've read your book. So ask your friends to read, to proofread your book and give you advice and feedback to make it better. You can also ask them to write a review if you can get them. So, do you have supportive friends who will support you in this endeavor? If you do not have supportive friends, but you really want to write a book, you can still get it published. You can do it by bringing yourself before the Lord and ask that He give you courage, like King David did when his army was against him.

It is possible, you and the Lord, to have a good relationship, but it's also helpful to have supportive friends when you take on the endeavor of writing a book. So have friends around you who support, encourage and ask you how you're doing in the process of writing a book. Don't be afraid to share with your friends what the book is about and even give them a glimpse of what you've finished and what you're going to add later. The more people you can get around you to encourage you in your effort, the better.

7. Do you have money to spend?

Some of the biggest publishers in the Christian book market require you to buy 1 or 2 thousand books if you publish. I could publish my books through Destiny Image, for instance, if I bought 2,000 books. Now, I don't know if they charge $5.00 a book, but it would probably cost me no less than $10,000 to publish my books through Destiny

Image. Unless I just wanted to sit on 2,000 books, I'd have to sell a lot of those 2,000 books to get my money back before I get royalties from Destiny Image. My best book has sold about 2,000 copies as an eBook and probably 250 copies as a paperback book. That's my best performing book, so it takes a while to recoup $10,000. I probably would have made about $1,000 on that book so far, which means I'd have to be 10 times as successful to get my $10,000 back.

Destiny Image and other publishers that ask you to buy 1,000 or 2,000 books are great for people who have great ministries, those who get around travelling from place to place and stadium to stadium, conference to conference. People could use these places for speaking about the book, maybe have a book table and sell their own books there every time they go. They may have 1,000 people in the audience and 50 people buy one of their books. And while it would take 20 times to sell a thousand books, that's okay for them.

I know a publisher that I'll mention further on in the book. This link I have publishes Christian books for people. The catch is compared to Destiny Image, you certainly have got to pay for your own editing. Once you're done with that, the link will distribute your books and possibly get them into book stores. It certainly gets them in eBook retailers all around the world and it's the one I use.

If you don't have the time to do it on your own, you have to pay someone else to do the editing. A book needs editing. So, do you have money to spend? If I said that it might cost you up to $1,000 to publish a book, do you have $1,000? Can you save up $1,000 or get a loan for $1,000 and pay it back to publish a book? You can publish a book cheaply. I know someone who spent about $50 publishing their book. It was quite a good book. It cost her $15 for the cover and nothing for Create Space. I don't know how she did it, but somehow, you can do it for free with Create Space. So it didn't cost her a lot. She's a good editor so I didn't notice any typos in her book. Sometimes, it's good to have a good copy editor to go through, rewrite, and polish your work. It also pays having a good proof-reader at your disposal to polish your work further.

If you add up all those services together, the cost of editing and publishing could sometimes add up to about $1,000 by the time you get a cover and everything.

Do you have money to spend? Can you get money to spend, because it's going to cost you money? Are you willing to put that money forward to do something that you want to do?

You may be able to get a copy editor that will cost you less. You may decide that your writing is good enough and you don't need a copy editor. I know that every book published by a reputable book publisher has a professional editor go through it. You owe it to your future readers to make it easier for them to read your book, something that only proper editing can produce.

8. Do you want to change someone's world?

Is there a person out there who is going to take your message and be transformed? When I was producing book one of my life's story, "His Redeeming Love," I was faced with the prospect of producing a book without a good ending, and I was fearful that people would think badly of me because of it. I only got over it by thinking that if the book can't change a lot of people, I'll just have to focus in changing at least one person's life with it.

Before I started writing, I thought about it. Is my book really going to greatly effect one person? Is one person going to be really inspired and wait for book two? Am I going to change his or her life? Is spending $500 to $1,000 worth it just to change one life? Would you spend that sort of money to change a person's life?

There are some books that have touched and changed my life. Do you want to change a life of one of your readers that badly? Would you really go to all the effort of writing a book, having it edited, proofread and published just to change one person's life? If yes, then think about that one person as you sit down to write your book. Picture that person in your mind as you start to write. Think about how you could make that person laugh, make that person cry, challenge that person and change them. Think about that kind of reader as you write, that one reader who is going to read your book and be changed.

9. Would you spend $1,000 to change 10 people's lives?

Are there people in your life who are bound by legalism and bound by rules and rule keeping? Do they think of an angry, judgmental God and always think and talk about the end times and how angry God is with people who sin? Is there a person like that where you wish you could give $100 and totally transform that person's life and set them free, have that person be happy and joyful and not think of a vengeful God? Would you spend that $100 for the life of that person that you love?

Well, it's the same as this: would you spend $1,000 of your own money to publish a book that will change 10 people's lives, 10 people who are loved by someone? Maybe not 10 people you know, but 10 people who are loved by someone the same way you love your friend. Would you change 10 people's lives for $1,000?

I know I would. I would do that all day. I would do it because I have a great understanding of eternal rewards. I know it means a lot more than $100 to the Lord to have someone's life changed. The Lord wants to impact everyone. So would you spend $1,000 only to have two of your books sold every month, equating to 24 books in a year? And if, say, half the people read the book and 5 people were really impacted, would you wait 2 years of your book sales at that slow pace to impact 10 people? Would it be worth it to you?

This is a question you have to ask yourself. I'm not saying your book is only going to impact 10 people, but would you do it for 10? Would you spend $1,000 to reach 10 people? Abraham asked God if he would spare the city of Sodom if there were 50 people who were righteous. And then he asked for 20, but finally settled for 10 people. God said He would spare the city if there were 10 righteous. But there weren't 10 righteous and God destroyed the city. But would you do it for 10? Would you spend $1,000 into this project to transform 10 people's lives? What if they had a certain life up until they read your book and then their life was changed forever? Would you write your book and pay to publish for it to change 10 people's lives?

That's the sort of question you want to ask yourself when you're thinking and considering if you want to write to change 10 people's lives, or even one. I know when I eventually get to Heaven, there'll be a lot of rewards for me, but there'll also be a lot of rewards for Joseph Prince because of what he did to my life. There'll be a reward for him for having influenced my life and many others with *"Destined to Reign."* Andrew Wommack affects millions of people around the world, but he'll certainly get a reward for having an impact on my life. Would you do it for one person? Would you do it for me? Would you spend $1,000 to change my life, to impact me?

10. Is earning money your motivation for writing your book or teaching people?

What's your motivation for writing the book that you want to write? Do you want to write a book and make money from writing books or do you want to change people's lives? Do you just want to change one person, two? Maybe 50 lives in a year from the sale of your book?

Let me explain using my book, "Prophetic Evangelism Made Simple." I know that if just one person captures the essence of that book and learns to evangelize prophetically like I can, I would have done something amazing. When I used to go out about 5 days a week from my house, I used to affect about 20 people a week with a prophetic message. If I shared that with one person through the book and one person did the same thing, it would be another 20. To spread the word even further, I made that book free in Kindle last month. Within that timeframe, 157 people downloaded the book. This month, only 4 people have bought it, but I still get excited when I think about how many people downloaded it last month. Even if there's a chance that only 15 people out of that 157 applied the lessons from that book, I've done a tremendous job. I get so excited about building fruit, building foundation in people that they can go and duplicate, that they can go and prosper in their Christian life because of something I've written.

I have 8 books published at the moment and I make between $150 to $200 a month. From those 8 books, I manage to make $12 from "Prophetic Evangelism" alone. That's not a lot of money to be making when you've put $1,000 into it. $12 a month would take 100 months, so it would take almost 10 years to recoup the $1,000 spent on that book, money which was spent for getting it transcribed and edited.

So what's your motivation? Do you want to write books to make money? There are a lot of books out there saying how you can make a lot of money in eBooks. However, this leads to having a lot of people pump out books that are unsatisfactory, just to make money. There are some who manage to make attractive titles, get good reviews on their books and make some money in the long run. I'm not saying money's a bad thing. I'm certainly looking forward to the time when I'm more popular in the world and my books are making $500 a month. But then ask yourself: is your motivation to make money or to change lives?

You have to look at your motivation. If your motivation is to make money, you might be sadly disappointed with how few sales you might get. One of my works, the first book of "His Redeeming Love," used to sell one copy a month. There are even months where I wasn't able to sell any copy at all. By selling one copy a month, I earn $3, which is a small amount compared to the $1000 I spent to publish it. Thus, in terms of making money out of it, the book was a big failure.

"His Redeeming Love" by far was my most expensive book because it had 103 chapters, all of which had to be transcribed and copy edited. It was an enormous book and it cost me a lot of money to make. But it's one of my favorite books because it's my life and it's transparent and I know it's going to touch the one person who reads it. It's going to touch, change and make in impact on individual lives. I wouldn't swap it for anything. I have other books that are more successful and that are starting to make me money, but it'll take a while before I get back all the money that I've spent.

You have to look at that motivation. If your motivation is to make money, I hope that you have 5,000 friends on Facebook and you can get a lot of traction in books sales through people you know. Of course, if you're a successful minister and you travel and speak once a week at different locations, self-publishing your book can make you some money. However, if your chief motivation was to make money, you need to think twice about writing a book. True enough, you can make money out of it. But I don't believe it should be your chief motivation.

11. Would you do it just to give your book away?

Here's something I'll probably cover later, but I want to share. For the last 2 and a half years, I've managed to keep my book, "The Parables of Jesus Made Simple," free to download every month. Depending on how the algorithm works in Amazon, sometimes in 2 days, 500 people download the book, sometimes only 50 people. On one 2-day session, 1,700 people downloaded the book.

Would you make your book available to be for free on Kindle for 5 days in every 90 days period? If you choose not to publish your book in other eBook retailers and use Kindle as your only eBook retailer, then through Create Space and Kindle Select Program, you can give your book away for 5 days every 90 days. My "Parables of Jesus Made Simple" is in the program and every month, I give it away for 2 days and every third month, I give it away for 1 day. So for 5 days every 3 months, I've given away about 10,000 copies of that book and that excites me so much.

I know a lot of people download books for free, but end up not reading them at all. Even if only 20% read it that would be 2,000 people who have been affected by that book. It's hard to read that book and not be convinced to walk in the commands of Jesus and walk in the way that He told us to live our lives. I don't pull punches in it. I tell people what Jesus actually meant in the book.

Would you publish a book so Kindle could allow you to give your book away and have 100 people download your book every month? Would you get excited about that? Would you spend $1,000 to give your book away for free? I know that when you have other books, if you give one book away, it actually advertises those other books for free. Thus, people would not only download your book, but some percentage of people could look at all the books you've written. This leads to the off-chance that someone would become interested in buying one of your books. I always do that, but it's ultimately your choice. Would you spend $1,000 to reach 10 people by sales per year or take the risk to reach out to 1,000 more by giving your book away?

It all comes back to your motivation in writing. Do you want to change people? Do you want to make money? Or do you want to do both? Of course, you can do both; I'm not saying you can't. Two months ago, I got a payment check from both the United Kingdom and American Kindle sales, for a grand total of $360 in a month. From my experience, it is possible to make money out of books. But again, ask yourself: would you write your book so people could get it for free? Would you get excited about that?

12. Do you feel God is calling you to write?

Do you feel that your desire to write is a calling by God on your life to write? Do you feel that it is what God wants you to do? I know that I'm called to preach. One time in the future, I'll be preaching in pulpits and churches. I'll be showing and teaching things to people. I have 1,300 videos on YouTube alone, so I'm certainly preaching already. Another thing that I know is that there are times when I'm called to write. There are times when I'm called to make books and educate people through books.

God may have been calling you for many years. You may have had God putting the thought into your mind for years. Maybe now, you are getting close to writing your first book, and you are picking up this book to read about what to do. I pray that as you read this book, you will come to realize that witting a book is not as hard as some people make it out to be. What is certain is the fact that if you are called to write one, maybe multiple books, you will not feel fulfilled until you begin to write them.

As a writer, you may never know when you are going to be inspired. I had the stirring today to make videos. I've made videos lots of times so it's not a big thing. All I need is the inspiration. I started to write a book on how to self-publish about a year ago, but I never finished it. I just didn't feel inspired to finish the book. Now, within one day, within a few hours, I've made the first draft of a book simply by being inspired. I was called to do it, and I have all the information I need for it. There seems to be quite a few books out there on this topic and yet I thought, seeing as God inspired me, He compelled me to make a use for it.

Do you feel a calling on your life to write? Have people prophesied to you that you are to write? Have you had a feeling that you should write? God could be calling you and it might not be just one book that He has in mind for you. You may be writing a whole host of books that are going to change people's lives. If you have a look at Bill Vincent on Amazon, my publisher, you will see he has up to 90 books that he has written. I believe Joyce Meyer has about 70 books so far. Your first book might be just the very start of your career.

13. Is there a message that you just have to share?

Jeremiah, the prophet, once spoke of wanting to share a message to the world, a message that was "like a flame within his bones that he had to get out, lest it consume him." Do you have such a message that you want to share to the world? Is there such a fire that burns within you? A fire that inspires you to share a message that you believe the world needs to hear?

Is there a message in you that pushes you to make necessary sacrifices just so people could hear it? Is there a message that you'd be willing to spend $1,000 for just so an audience as small as 10 people to be impacted? Is it a message that needs to be said and no one but you could say it the way it is intended to be said?

Do you have the knowledge? Do you have the wisdom? Do you have inspiration? Do you have directions from God? Do you have nuggets of wisdom from God's throne room that you have to share with people? Are you passionate about something and you want to share your passion with other people? If you answer yes to all of these, then you have very good reasons to write a book. If you have something within you that you just can't contain and want to share to the rest of the world, you have the reason to write a book.

With that said, I leave you with two things: this book, which shares every personal point I have on how to write and publish a book; and videos that serve as companion pieces for this book. Everything that you will need to make that first book is here, all the information gathered from my own experiences in honing the craft. By going through the following pages of this book and through the videos, I hope that you will eventually learn the technique and the understanding of how to write and publish in the same way as I did.

May God bless you and keep you safe. Amen

Section 2
29 Tips to writing your book - the process of writing

Tip 1 - Getting Inspiration

Inspiration is a funny thing. There are times when inspiration comes to you out of nowhere, or when you least expect it. As an aspiring writer, you certainly can't write a book without inspiration. For example, I'm sure there are some people out there who one day thought that, "I want to write a book or a couple of chapters about the Book of Revelation!" They'll probably go through the trouble of doing a whole lot of research, talking to the right people, and eventually coming up with the book, only to find out too late that the book is of bare-bones quality.

See the problem here? Doing research is well and good, but unless the Lord has inspired you to write something on the Book of Revelation, it won't come out well. First of all, learn the habit. As an aspiring writer, it's easy to start by writing articles and blog posts just to get the habit of writing regularly. Fill in your time writing on certain subjects and themes and keep your creative juices flowing until the inspiration for something larger appears.

For example, I wasn't aware until today that I was going to do a couple of videos. I wasn't sure what they were going to be about and I had to wait for inspiration to kick in. The first inspiration came with the first video that I did, which was "Tips to getting your book published." I did a video with a number of points, focusing on 11 tips on self-publishing books. The video became the second of three videos that I did, and they became this book called "Writing and Publishing Christian Non Fiction."

Remember, the first thing that you need when writing is to have the inspiration. If you don't have the inspiration for your book, you do not have a book. There's no use trying to sit down and say you're going to write a book on a certain subject if you do not have that overall feeling of love and passionate desire to write something.

An hour after having done two videos, I proceeded to make a third and it eventually became the first part of this book. The second video I did became this section, which is the second part to the book. Finally, the first video I did ended up as the third part of this book. It just shows that sometimes you might not know how your book is going to turn out until you've finished writing it all. When I sat down to do the first video, I thought that was all it was going to be. However, when I got inspiration for the second video, I thought I could turn my work into a short helpful eBook. By the time I did the third video, I was quite sure that I was going to have a good sized little book that was going to be very helpful for its readers.

If you've made the decision to write, always wait for that inspiration to kick in. It'll always be worth the wait.

Tip 2 - Does the idea have "legs"?

Is the idea that you've thought of good enough to make 50 pages? Is it enough for 80 pages? How about 200 pages? Most people would enjoy a book that reads up to or over 80 pages. Fewer than that really isn't something substantial. While this little eBook might be less than 80 pages, I find the length justified since all it contains is information that's straight to the point. I imagine you could crank up the page count on the process of writing and self-publishing a book by putting a lot of fluff and extra material into it. That should definitely push the page count to about, say, 200 pages or more.

When I ask if your book, your idea, has "legs," all I'm asking is, "are you happy with how long your book is going to be?" The length of your book is its foundation. Would you be able to make an 80-page book out of what you're producing? Does your idea have enough substance to make something that will be comprehensive, enjoyable, interesting, and teach people a certain amount of information about it?

There's a chance that some of your ideas may seem good, inspired even. But not every idea can have legs. Not every idea can have enough material that'll give it substance. Some of those ideas may be something that you can probably cover in just five pages, and you certainly would be hard pressed in publishing a book and getting people to buy with that kind of material. So you have to ask yourself: "does my idea have legs?" Does my idea have enough substance in it that will produce a book that will be over 40, 50, 80 pages? Will it be substantial enough? See the thing is, if your idea does not have enough legs, if it does not have enough substance to it, in the end, you can say it's a good idea, but it's not good enough for you to make a book about it.

Of course, there's always an exception. For instance, a book that's only 40 pages long could be considered as a sparse book. But if you manage to write those 40 pages in a manner that makes it really informative and understandable to the reader, then that becomes a very good book. While this sounds contradictory from what I said earlier, this only shows that it's possible for you to write a short book if that book has an idea that is substantial enough. The quality and substance of the book justifies people into spending money for it. It justifies having them give good reviews for it, even have them say that "That was an excellent book!" Thus, your idea must be substantial enough to justify that page count. If the idea does not justify the need to create a book for it, then what's the point?

Tip 3 - Book title & Chapter titles.

I've basically covered this third tip in "How to Self-Publish a Book," but let me talk further about the process. After I've decided to write a book, I'll search in my mind for a book title. Once I think of one that adequately describes what the book is going to be about, I grab a pad of paper, sit down and start jotting down the first 20 or 30 or 40 chapter titles that comes in my head. For instance, I sat down before I did this video and wrote all the tips down. Through the course of my writing, I also jotted down the book title and chapter titles in a page where I was writing one tip. From there, I could write two A4 pages worth of content for each chapter I made. When I transfer them on a 6 by 9 book, it instantly becomes 4 pages.

Just to put things in perspective, if you want a book to be about 160 pages, you'd probably need 40 chapter titles, with content worth two A4 pages each. If you convert that to the same book size I'm using, then that two pages worth of content becomes 4 pages. Same goes with an 80 page book. For just 20 chapters you could double the size of your draft into a very good little book. And all of this is just thanks to the book's page size.

The way to work on your book title and the actual idea of the book, the way to work out whether your book has legs or not is to sit down and write those chapter titles. Each of the chapter titles has to adequately describe what is going to be said in that chapter. You'll want to build a foundation at the beginning of the book for what you're going to be saying later on in the book. Each of the chapter titles should be able to stand-alone, but at the same time be part of the whole package. By reading the chapter titles, your reader should get a progressive revelation of what the book is talking about, even if a chapter should talk about a specific aspect of your book's subject

By the time you've written most of your chapter titles, it should be clear to you what your book's going to say. Writing most of your book's chapter titles is also a sort of test to see if your work has the foundation or the "legs" to make it stand as an actual book. If it doesn't have "legs," you'll find that it will be difficult for you to write more than five chapter titles of your work. That certainly isn't long enough for a book.

Let me tell you this, it's quite all right to write a book out of inspiration, even if it doesn't have "legs." It happens to me quite often enough, more so with this book. Since this book deals with a subject that many people have already written on, I'm sure those books have great things to say. But even so, I still felt compelled to make a couple of videos about the subject and share it with the people I know. And since it doesn't take too much effort to have the videos transcribed in paper and edited to make a short eBook out of it, then why shouldn't I make one and share it as well?

I've found that I have a little bit of a following now. People who have read my books like to look at and read my other books, so I already know how many readers are going to look forward to what I have to say in my future works. They say that every person out there has a book within them that's just waiting to be written, so this short eBook is something that will certainly be helpful to the average person who has aspirations in writing that one book, one day.

Write the chapter headings. Make sure they progress, one on top of the other. It's quite okay to just have 26 or 28 chapter titles the same way this section of the book has. You don't have to force yourself in adding two more chapters just to pad things out. It's actually more believable, more credible and more authentic to have a number that sounds not rounded out. As you progress through the book, an opportunity may yet come to you to add in another chapter title just because you've found that something else has to be said. Just keep writing and wait for inspiration to hit you. Don't force yourself to add in a new chapter if it's not necessary.

Tip 4 - Reflect on the subject.

Take some time to meditate on the subject that you're going to write about. Take some time to pray on it, to think about it. Let it stew with you for a few days or weeks. You can even reflect on it and think about it before you write your chapter titles. Think around the subject and think of what you'll say about it. Try to get some ideas from some of the illustrations that you'll use, or from some of the stories that you're going to use. Just meditate on it and let the idea marinate like meat that's put on the fridge for a day or two. Let it get flavor in your mind so that you have a real idea of the feeling and the information that you want your book to express.

Reflect on the subject. Picture your idea marinating like meat in the fridge and how exquisite it'll taste when it's cooked and all the flavors are infused. Some of the things you think about, some of the ideas and concepts you get while you're meditating on the subject are going to give the book its flavor. If you rush out and do the book straight away, you might not get the added flavor and texture that the book might have got had you reflected on it further.

Tip 5 - Ask people about the subject.

While you're busy "marinating" on your book's subject, one of the best things you could do is to talk to other people about it. Go on Facebook, for instance, and say, "I'm thinking of writing a book on this. Here are a few of the chapter titles. What are your suggestions? What would you like to see in the book?" If you have friends who love you and care about you, they'll post what they want to see in that book and what they like it to achieve. This approach is so much helpful when you've already written a book, but it is also very helpful at this stage since you can get some concepts and ideas that you haven't considered before. You might even find that you can write a few chapter titles based on what was asked for or what your friends suggested.

Remember that normal people are going to be reading your book, and it would be very thoughtful and interesting to ask them for suggestions and ask what they'd like to read about in the future. It may be something simple that people want to know. For instance, they could ask me why I don't think the Antichrist is going to be here for another 20 years. That would be an interesting thing to talk about. And I have detailed structured points why I say that this is the case. If I was going to write a book on the end times, the Mark of the Beast and the Antichrist and why I think he's not going to arrive for the next 20 years, they may ask for detailed reasons why I think that's the case. That's just an example of something people may want to know.

Now it may be natural to you, it may be a given that you know that is the case. But your readers wouldn't know that. They don't know your inner workings. They don't know the understandings that you have about the Antichrist and how long it's going to be before he comes here. They'll want to know it in detail and they'll want to know the reasoning behind your thoughts. You have to give your readers a chance to request what they want to read in your book. You might discard or not even bother with some of the things that they'll say, but a lot of what they say may be confirming what you've already decided to put into the book. When that happens, you'll know that you're on the right track.

Tip 6 - Ask God to help you write.

It's amazing to know that there are a lot of Christian writers out there who manage to write a book without necessarily including God in the writing process. You might be a person who thinks that God supports everything you do. A lot of Christians decide what they're going to do and then ask God to bless it. The best way, however, is to ask for God's guidance and then do what He tells you. If you have the courage, ask God if it was his idea for you to write a book, and if yes, ask him to help you write it. If you happen to be inspired, then there's a good chance it was God's idea for you to write. Pray a prayer specifically to God that He would lead you, guide you and help you as you write. You'll find that just as the Holy Spirit is helping me with this book that I'm making, God will help you and anoint you as you write.

There's a difference between certain Christian books. Some have less impact to the person reading them. There are, however, certain Christian books that'll emit a strong presence of God when you read them. The presence of God will be so strong, it'll be just like reading the Bible. That's when you know that the book you're holding is anointed. Anointed books are those that have been co-written with the Holy Spirit. It's as if the Holy Spirit has guided the person as he or she wrote the book and allowed God's anointing to carry through with the book. That's the kind of presence you'll want your book to have, and the way to do that is to ask Him to help you to write.

Tip 7 - Write your first chapter.

When you start writing your first chapter, remember that you set your own limits. If you can only write the content of one chapter to one page, you might end up making a book with 40 one-page chapters. If that happens to be your hindrance, your limitations as a writer, then work with it. At this point, it's best to remember not to over-write. Don't write fluff. Don't write pointless paragraphs to fill the page. Write succinctly. Write as if you meant every word. Write the subject as you see fit, but don't try and pad it in any way. Write as much as you can say about the subject in a concise manner.

This is one of the reasons why it's important to write out the chapter titles at the beginning. You'll want to work out what you're going to say in two pages before you write. When you're writing your chapter titles and see something that's going to take four A4 pages, you'll want to split it to two chapters to keep your book format.

Remember that you set your own limits when it comes to writing. There is no rule that once you're done writing one chapter, you'll have to wait until the next day to write it. If you're excited to write the next chapter and you have the time to do it, then do so. Also, I suggest that for every time you finish writing a chapter, you go back and reread it. Edit and proofread it if needed. Once you've done that, it'll be easier for you to sit down and write your second chapter.

There was this one book where I wrote nine chapters in one sitting. And when I got back to it, I wrote five chapters in two sittings. I wrote that 19 chapter book in three sittings. The thing is its okay to write more than one chapter in a sitting. You can write four or five if you like. I do not have a full time job at the moment so I have a lot of time on my hands. This means I can stay up from 8 o'clock in the evening until 4 in the morning doing nothing but writing. Of course, not everyone has that luxury, especially if they have a full time job. But if you think you can write fast enough to go past the number of chapters you usually write per day, then by all means, go for it.

It's not every day that a writer feels excited about his work. If you're not excited to write the second chapter, you don't have to do it straight away. But then again, if you're not excited to write the second chapter, what are you writing? Is the message you're writing for other people? Is the message you're writing going to be enjoyable to other people? If you can't get excited about writing your second chapter, is there something seriously wrong with your first chapter? This is a very important question that you need to take seriously, because if you're not interested in what you're writing, then why should people feel otherwise? Believe me. You have to be excited about what you're writing about, because your excitement shows how interesting your book is going to be. You may have to think about another chapter title or another subject to write about and rewrite your first chapter. At this point, when you make the change, you should be excited to get on and write your second chapter.

Tip 8 - Don't edit as you write, edit after you write.

Some people think that once they've written a paragraph, they should stop writing just so they could edit, fine tune, and rewrite it. While editing and proofreading is a must to ensure that the quality of your book is satisfactory, it's advisable that you write the whole chapter before you go back and do that. Don't stop and make everything perfect as you write the chapter. While being aware in using proper punctuation and proper use of grammar is a must while writing, don't use it as an excuse to backtrack. Get it all written down first, and don't try to touch anything until you do so.

Some people might never finish a book because they become stuck in the process of editing their initial chapters. They want it to look so perfect in the first few pages that they never get around to writing the entirety of it. I'm told that Stephen King edits his book about 13 times, polishes each paragraph and changes and edits his book. I'm told Bryce Courtney who was an Australian, did it about 20 times in his book (he has since passed away).

There's time for editing and there's time for writing. When you write, get everything down in paper first. I don't think Stephen King polishes every paragraph as he writes it. He's a good writer and he probably does write good paragraphs from the get go. But he also improves upon it by rereading his work 13 times. Just be sure to understand that if the professionals do it like that, then why do things differently? Stephen King, I think, is the largest and the most popular bookseller in the world, certainly the number one author on Amazon. And I'm sure, as a fellow writer, he would advise you not to get stuck editing your work before you have it down on paper, just as I would advise you not to.

Tip 9 - Read your chapter, fix the errors, and take your time to edit where you can.

When you've finished writing your chapter, take the time to read it. Fix the typos. Fix the spelling mistakes. Take your time to edit where you can. Personally, I'm not fantastic at English. You may be able to tell when you watch my video that my words aren't the biggest words in the world. Thankfully, I have a tremendously good copy editor who polishes my words and makes my words sound really good. My copy editor does a good job in transforming my words into something that's pleasing to read and hear. I come up with the initial subject matter and I write down the initial words on a page. She then comes along and polishes what I've written. Essentially, she rewrites and edits the book, but she doesn't write it for me. It's still my job to put things down on paper. It's still my job to make sure that I reread each chapter and fix the grammar and spelling as best as I could. This is to ensure that she could understand what I'm saying and rewrite it into something that looks more polished and professional. She does such a supernatural job to my work that when I re-read it, it's as if what's written still sounds like me, yet it's not. It looks polished and it looks wonderful, but to me it still sounds as if I wrote it. That's the purpose of a really good copy editor.

Tip 10 - Read your last chapter before you write the next to create momentum.

Before you sit down to write a new chapter, make sure to go back and read a preceding chapter or two to create momentum. Read what you've already done and get into the momentum. Get into the flow of what you've said, and use that momentum to kick start your next chapter.

This was a trick I used when I sat down and wrote the nine chapters of *"Your Identity in Christ."* Since the four chapters I've finished beforehand were still fresh in my mind, it gave me enough momentum to finish writing chapter five. I used this trick again to great effect when I went to write the next five chapters in the second sitting.

That's one tip I'd like to share, to help create momentum in your writing and help you get things done in a very proficient and timely manner. Otherwise, you might end up having what some people would refer to as "writer's block." Another way to cure writer's block is to be inspired, to have a book that's got "legs." If your book has a strong foundation and you're inspired, make sure that you also read a chapter or two before you start to write your next chapter. That way, you'll never be affected by writer's block.

Tip 11 - If you don't know an exact quote, just say "I heard it."

There are times when, during the course of my writing, I want to say something by quoting someone. Trouble is, there are times when I can't remember who said it or what book and page number they said it. If that happens, you can just say, "It's been said before" and then quote what is said. If you know the name of the person, but you don't know or remember where you heard or read it, you can say, "I heard Matthew Robert Payne say this once in one of his teachings" and then say it. With this, at least, you're giving the person credit, even if you can't recall where you've heard or read it.

Truth be told, I don't get so worried about that. I know that the person said it. I know that I remember it. Don't get too hung up about having to cite exact quotes, exact page numbers and book names to quote that person. I'm sure people quote me from time to time and probably wouldn't remember where they got it. They just know that I said it once, and there's a good chance that someone else said it and I was just quoting them.

Don't get hung up about that. Most of the time, your audience wouldn't care where you got the quote. The only thing they need is to understand what you're saying. And to do that, they need you to reinforce and establish your point using a quote. That's the importance of quotes. Some editors might really get upset with me saying that. I had a copy editor once who frustrated me because I couldn't quote anything unless I cited the exact source of the quote. Eventually, I got so fed up that I didn't use her services again.

Don't take things too seriously. Learn to feel comfortable in quoting what you can quote and remembering what you can remember.

Tip 12 - Be transparent.

I try to be transparent in everything I do and say all the time. I like to use examples in what I say. For instance, let's go back to when I said that I don't believe that the Antichrist is coming within the next 20 years. That's something I believe personally. I don't believe Jesus will be here within the next 20 years. There are too many things that need to be done before He can come back. All these worries about the Mark of the Beast and all this stuff doesn't worry me because it's not that his mark's coming out anytime soon. That's an example of being transparent. By saying something that counts as my personal opinion, by saying something that's personal and dear to me, I become transparent.

I had a friend who saw the Antichrist in a vision 10 years ago. He was about 23 back then. That's an example of being transparent. By saying that I know someone and telling what I've heard and what I personally believe, there's a chance I can get myself into trouble. If I said that to the whole world on a news broadcast, there would be millions of people clamoring for my head and saying, "Don't you know He's coming back in the next 5 years?" Everyone has their opinion on the book of Revelation. To be transparent is to share your life, to share your stories with people, to be vulnerable. When you share that you had a 20 year addiction like I had to other people, everyone who has ever had an addiction will connect with you. These people will suddenly feel, "I'm at home with you because you're real and you're honest." And people who never had an addiction would be impressed that you could be so honest. You win these people to yourself. People will believe you the more you become transparent. It's one of the laws in marketing and influence: the law of candor. Candor means telling the truth. The law of candor states that if you say something that is embarrassing or potentially embarrassing about yourself, people will believe you more because of your honesty. And through your honesty, they start to believe you, even when it's clear that you're trying to impress something upon them.

I don't always use it for that reason. Still, it doesn't change the fact that, as a person, I'm just transparent and honest. As an aspiring writer, you should try to be transparent. Don't just write and make a point. Use an example out of your life; use a story out of your life even if it is embarrassing. I had an addition for 20 years and I never thought that I could stop that addiction. It was just so wired into me. Even so, I managed to break it through the power of Jesus Christ and through the power of repentance. Christ is real. He really is real and He can transform your life. If you want to talk about addictions or compulsive habits and how the power of Jesus can heal or break them, you could use that example. By using an example of your life, you reinforce your words and make them believable. People can argue with facts, but they can't argue with testimony. Being transparent builds belief in people. Don't just make your points. Don't just write about stuff that you know about. Use illustrations and be transparent when you do.

Tip 14 - Use your own stories first and then use other people's stories.

When you're illustrating your points and you have a choice between your story and someone else's story, use your story. Of course, you could use someone else's story if that story happens to be the best story that illustrates your point. But still, try and use your stories as often as you can. Try and make your work flow in a way that allows someone to learn not only about the subject, but also learn a little more about you. The more they get to know you, the more they'll trust that what you're saying is true. The best way to make that happen is to write about subjects that you know. For instance, I don't do research on any of the subjects of my books. I write about the things that I know, so I illustrate all of my points with personal stories, anecdotes and personal illustrations because I know the subject so well. It's so close to my heart that I'm able to illustrate each of my points through my experiences alone.

I've had so many people write to me about my books and say that I'm so transparent and so honest that they just love everything I have to say. By reading every book I've produced, by reading the stories told in them, they've grown to love me for it. All of us might not remember the commands of Jesus and the things that he taught us to do and not to do. But so many of us remember the story of the Prodigal Son, the Good Samaritan, the Lost Sheep, even the Parable of the Lost Coin. We remember His stories because people love stories. So tell your stories as often as you can.

Tip 15 - Use your best illustration to make your point.

Use the best stories to illustrate your points. Don't go out of your way to talk about yourself so much that you use your entire life story in the process. If there's a good story about someone else's life and it illustrates your point perfectly, use that story. I use illustrations that I've heard from other preachers that perfectly illustrate my point. When I'm co-writing with the Holy Spirit, when the Holy Spirit is giving me utterance as I write, He directs me to the story that would best illustrate my point. I'm not afraid to open and use any illustration to prove and illustrate my point. I'm not afraid to back away from sharing that I had an addiction for 20 years because it appropriately and perfectly illustrates my point that you have to be transparent. Of course, some people would say that's not the sort of subject matter that you should put in a book about how to write books. But it's a perfect illustration about being transparent. People would really be impressed that you're able to share your life experience to illustrate your points and not be afraid. If it reinforces your point and gets it across to your readers, then what is there to fear?

To summarize: use yourself as an example to illustrate the points that you make and use the best stories. But if there's a story about someone else that illustrates your point perfectly, then use that story. Make it your goal to teach people about a certain subject, but let them learn about you in the process. The more they learn about you, the more they will be encouraged to look up your other works, either through Amazon or other places that sell your works. Don't be afraid to put yourself into the story.

Tip 16 - Remember that people love personal stories.

A friend of mine who I used to write articles for contacted me one day. He knew that I had the gift of prophecy and asked if I could give him a foretelling of his future. When I was done, he asked me if I could also do the same to his sister, and to another one of his sisters after that. Then, after I did my part he said, "I notice you speak about visiting Heaven. Do you think you can get a message from my mother?" I complied and, after envisioning a scene where his mother sat and dictated her message to Jesus, I then wrote a letter containing her message. My friend then showed it to his sisters and they wept. They wept because they were so blown away by how the message felt as if it was their mother talking to them instead of me talking. A year or so later, this friend wrote to me and said he had a dream of the Antichrist. He had three consecutive dreams about the Antichrist for over a year now, so he could vividly remember what he looked like. He told me about the Antichrist's age, what he looked like, learned that he was in middle level government and all sorts of things. I learned all of that through him, from having a personal relationship with him and prophesying over him. I know beyond a doubt that Jesus showed him the Antichrist. I know that everything I did lead me to this moment, as if it was preordained, as if it was meant to happen.

Don't you love a personal story? That was a personal story. That was one of my stories. I don't believe in anyone else's opinion of who the Antichrist is. I know who he is, how old he is and when he's coming. You can build on a personal story. People love personal stories. People love it when you illustrate your points with your personal stories. It's usually everyone's favorite part of the book. Don't let Satan tell you that you're talking about yourself too much. Don't let Satan get in your ear that they don't want to know about that. Don't listen to what he says. People like personal stories, and I, for one, get excited when someone illustrates a point with a personal story. People never tire of them. I have a book at home that was written by a healer containing 30 of his favorite healing stories. Basically, it's just one story after another, but I never get tired of reading them. My book, "His Redeeming Love," is just one story after another about my life. But people loved reading the book because it gives them an insight, a glimpse about my life. Be confident that people are going to enjoy reading your personal stories.

Tip 17 - Don't try and prove what you can't prove.

Don't try to force stuff on people. I can't personally prove that the Antichrist isn't coming back in the next 10 years, but I'm just very confident that he's not. There's so much stuff that's going to happen to the world before Jesus comes back that even if it happens now, it would take 10 years to make all of it come true. Despite my confidence, I don't go about trying to prove stuff that I can't prove. I live my life in repentance and humility. I live my life in the will of God and I'm ready for Jesus to come back at any time. People would often catch me saying I'd rather be in Heaven than be on earth. I know that I'm only here because I have a job to do and God wants me to do it. But personally, I'd rather be in Heaven. I feel like what Paul felt when he wrote the same thing. I'm ready for Jesus. I'm ready to meet God any day. I'm not saying that Jesus isn't coming back in the next 20 years because I'm not ready. I'm ready now. It's just that, as a prophet, I know so much about what's going to happen and how things are going to play out that I know that his return is not going to happen anytime soon.

Share your opinion and be humble about it. Be assertive about it only if you know the subject quite well, but don't use it as an excuse to try and push things down people's throats. Don't try and make them believe something that you do not have enough evidence for. Better to be humble about something than be dogmatic. Reassure people that what you say is only your opinion, especially when you're talking about a point that might be hard to prove.

Tip 18 - Be passionate with your subject, but don't be intense about it.

Be passionate. I know I was when I wrote and talked on my video about meeting that guy who saw the Antichrist in dreams, my interaction with him and his sisters, and the happiness I felt when he and his sisters gave their feedback about their letters. You might have picked from my example that I can be both passionate and a little intense about that subject.

Be passionate about your subject. If you're not passionate about your subject, then don't expect your reader to be passionate. Sweep them up like a wave that catches people and washes them ashore. Like a wave, pick people up with your writing and push them towards the direction you want them to go. Be passionate. Learn to be confident in yourself as you write. But try not to be intense about it.

Tip 19 - Don't judge yourself too hard.

It's true that most writers really are hard on themselves. They are their best and worst critic. You can be the most passionate in what you do and what you've achieved, and at the same time, be very critical about it. Don't be too hard on yourself. Just remember that at the end of the day, what you're writing is your opinion. Even though you may have plenty of scripture verses to back up what you're saying, even though plenty of writers in the New Testament have said similar things and have similar precepts and ideas, at the end of the day, it's your opinion about the truth.

I've heard people who taught about the law of God and how we have to obey the law and the Ten Commandments. I've heard them saying that we have to tithe, we have to read our Bible, we have to pray, and we have to do all these things and all these rules. I've heard people preach that so hard that I sucked it all up and I believed every single word. It made me a very intense and angry person. It made me believe in an angry God, a vengeful God whose actions were supported by scripture and doctrine. But then, I got saved by the message of grace, and I learned that God wasn't an angry God at all. I learned that the true God was perfectly expressed in the person of Jesus Christ. Through Jesus, the messages of grace and the supporting scriptures, I've become a whole lot happier. I felt as if I was set free by the message of grace.

I got a little bit intense with the message of grace as usual. I've come across people who were preaching extreme grace. They preached that you don't have to obey Jesus, that you can do anything and that you're forgiven for everything. You don't have to repent. You only have to repent once when you become a Christian. Then I found people using scriptures to support themselves, but nonetheless were teaching wrong things to other people. Everyone is teaching their opinion. If you go into some of the traditional churches, you'll find preachers who talk of law-based scripture that they believe to be true. And how could they not believe? They've been taught in Bible colleges to say that with 100 verses to support it and they believe that's the truth.

But at the end of the day, there is only one truth. The rest is just opinion.

Don't be too hard on yourself. At the end of the day, what you're saying is your opinion. Illustrate it with plenty of stories, be comfortable, and be easy on yourself. Relax. Don't judge yourself too harshly.

Tip 20 - Write from the heart, not from your mind.

Write from the heart. Write with emotion, with passion, with love. Don't try and convince people of what you're saying by being really analytical about it. Don't write solely with your mind. Write a summary of what you're going to say. Put some good music on. Listen to some anointed music and just let the words from your heart pour forth. Write from who you are, from your spirit, from the loving side of you. Think about that person who really needs your message. Think about writing a message that's going to affect and influence them in a big way. Write a message from your heart to their heart. Imagine them being transformed by your message. Think of that one person and try to connect with him or her. Try and write a message that brings a positive influence in their life.

Let's go back to my views about the coming of Jesus and the Antichrist. That's an example of how I speak from the heart. Whether you notice or not, I got pretty intense about the subject. And that intensity comes from the heart. If I thought about it too much and didn't speak from my heart, if I didn't speak from my emotion, I might have tempered what I said.

Write from your emotion. Write from the essence of who you are. Don't write to convince people of something you don't fully believe in yourself. If you can't prove something, don't try and prove it. Use your stories and say in your opinion. Don't do some big analytical thought process in trying to convince people. Sit down with your subject. Sit down with anointed music. Sit down with the help of the Holy Spirit and speak your mind. Speak your heart to the people, and you will do a good job.

Tip 21 - Enjoy yourself as you write and relax.

The writing experience isn't some intense, hard process. If you find that writing not enjoyable at all, then I'll have to question if you really want to be a writer or not. If you're not being too hard on yourself and you're writing from the heart, then you should be able to write easily. If you're writing from your mind and you want to convince people of something by using all the best phrases arguments you can find, then you might not enjoy yourself. Yes, writing isn't easy. There are no clear-cut rules when it comes to writing. But if you're open, if you're transparent, if you love what you're sharing and you're writing because you want to make an impact to people, then you'll enjoy yourself.

Don't put too much pressure on yourself. You might decide to write two chapters a week. If you miss one week and you didn't manage to write your two chapters, don't be too hard on yourself. Don't try and write four chapters the next week. Write what you can write.

Don't stress yourself. If you're worried about what you're writing and how you're writing, then that will come through as you write. If you're stressed, then people will feel the stress. Enjoy yourself. You don't have to publish the book. One concern that writers have is they're afraid of people judging their craft. They're afraid of getting something wrong. If you're going to teach and share something, but you're afraid of getting something wrong, then you'll never be able to start.

Take my books for instance. I'm certain that there are errors in nearly every book I've written. Am I worried about it? While there are certain things I wish I'd changed in one or two of my books, I don't beat myself up about it. Enjoy the process. If you enjoy the process, then your readers will certainly enjoy what you have to say in your work.

Tip 22 - Hire a good copy editor to do the extra work.

When you get professionally published, chances are you'll have an editor assigned to you. The editor's job is to tell you what you need to change in your book to make it more accessible to readers. Once you hear of the changes that you need to do, you can either start rewriting on your own, or hire someone to do it for you. This is where the copy editor comes in. When I hire a copy editor, I just give her the book and she rewrites and polishes it for me. I failed English and I'm not really good at it. So I trust that she knows what she's doing, since it's her job to polish my work. From time to time however, I find something that I think she did wrong and I rewrite it and don't send it back to her. Having a good copy editor prevents that from happening, and I know one that makes sure she gets everything right.

My copy editor's name is Melanie Cardano. She works at Upwork.com and comes highly recommended. She's a Christian editor who works at $16 an hour, a lot better than the Australian or American rate of $80 an hour.

Editing is really hard work, so it's best that you let a professional copy editor do the work for you. It's work that's only schooled for them. As a writer, you can't always see your own mistakes. And it's a fact that every book that has been published has at least gone through the hands of a copy editor. So don't feel that you're less of writer if your work ends up getting rewritten. While they're experts in what they do, it's still up to you to write what they have to fix. My copy editor, Melanie, certainly couldn't come up with the things I say in my books. Just like my mother who does copy editing for me, she tells me that she couldn't do what I do. But she can certainly transform it and change it into something that's more readable and has better grammar and spelling in it.

Let your copy editor do that extra work for you. Don't stress about what you have. Do your best to write down what you have and then let a copy editor do the rest.

Tip 23 - Share your manuscript with a friend or two.

Share your manuscript with a friend or two to get some feedback for free. With luck, you may even ask them to proofread it for you. Ask your friends on Facebook if they would be willing to proofread your manuscript and send them a copy so they could work on it quickly. And while you're at it, ask them if they could write a comment of what they thought about the book. Maybe you could even ask them to write a review for it on Amazon when it gets published.

It's important that you get some feedback on what you've actually written. If you're at a point when you've written a book and you're wondering how good it is or if it makes a good case for what you are teaching, but you feel afraid of what other people might say about it, this is a good time for you to get honest feedback from a friend. Just relax and share what you have with a friend or two and have them encourage you through their feedback. They'll see things in your book that you probably didn't see. They'll see how good you are as a writer and they'll give you the feedback that your heart wants to hear.

Remember, Satan's good at condemning and judging people. Remember that he's very good at using your own words and thoughts against you. Sometimes, it's very hard to distinguish between your thoughts and Satan's thoughts when it comes to your book. You may even end up being hard on yourself.

But when you open your book up to a couple of friends and ask them to give you feedback, it'll be like getting a fresh breeze of air. It's like a refreshing drink, a refreshing wave breaking over you that lets you know that you've done a tremendous job. It lets you know that your book is worthwhile, that it certainly has plenty of good points in it that you've expressed. Do it for your own sake. If you're not convinced, then do it for three reasons: One is for them to help you proofread it, two is to get a review and three is to get some feedback that will encourage you.

Tip 24 - Offer your manuscript free on Facebook for honest reviews of your friends.

Now that you have your manuscript copy edited, proofread and professionally ready, there's another thing that you can do: offer people your manuscript for free, and ask them if they can write a review for you. Make the offer on Facebook and, when you get a willing response, send them a word document of your book. Some of your friends may say that they'll read it, but probably won't go through with it. But with luck and with a little prayer, you should be able to find a couple of people who are willing to read and send you a review. If they're willing to send a review, ask them if they can post it on Amazon when the book gets published. Having people with an Amazon account to read and review it for you is a huge plus, so make sure that they have an account when you start asking them for reviews. If they do not have an account on Amazon, but they're willing to read it and give feedback, don't shy away from them. It won't cost you anything and sharing it with friends will give you good feedback and encouragement. Even if they do not have an Amazon account, it's helpful to get their feedback on your book.

Tip 25 - One more proofread

It never hurts to reread. Even once you get all the feedback from your friends and you've managed to have your book proofread, read the book once more. You'll be amazed how many errors you'll probably find in a book, even when people have copy edited and proofread it. With luck, you won't be able to encounter any error. But just to be safe and sure, go through your book and get the final touchups done.

Tip 26 - Publish it.

Now if you've followed tip no. 24, then your book is ready to be published. For this, you have a few options: you can either choose the Christian publisher that I use or use Create Space. My publisher does eBooks and puts my work in about 1,000 eBook retailers. He'll make sure that it's ready for bookstores to receive. As a bonus, he'll also do an audio book of your work. He'll publish it all for a good price.

Tip 27 - Stay positive.

If you manage to affect at least one person with your book, then you've done a good job. I remember when I was publishing the first part of my book "His Redeeming Love." I was going to publish it in two parts, but eventually, I published part one and then published the whole book rather than a part two. When I was publishing the first part, I agonized over publishing something that didn't have a good ending to the story. It was half way through my life when I still had my addiction, so it made sense that the book ended in a cliffhanger. I agonized over it until I came to the point where I thought: was it going to affect one person and change that person's life? Was it going to have a positive effect on one person?

When I have that one person in mind, I knew that if that person found out that there was going to be a book two coming out, chances are it would have encouraged that one person. It's important to remember that when you write, you write for that one person. Try and make a message that will appeal to that one person. Try to make them change their mind about life. Let them have emotions. Let them have an emotional change because of your book. It doesn't matter if your work isn't read by a lot of people. As long as you touch the life of at least one person, it'll be worthwhile.

You might find that you'll go through all the effort of publishing a book, only to have five people buy it on Kindle per month. You might get really depressed about that. But think of the possibility that two of those people could have their lives changed because of that book. Remember that one in a hundred people write a review on Amazon. Remember that you might not hear from every person who reads your book. It's really important that you share your book with friends and family and get their feedback, because it might be some time before you actually hear from someone who has bought and read your book.

There's also the possibility that a lot of people will read or have read your book. You might have 20 people per month reading your book, but only one out of those people will write to you. Not every person has the time or courage to write to an author and tell them that they really loved the book the author made. Instead of thinking what could be and what could've been, just be positive and think of that one person you can change.

Tip 28 - Celebrate your reviews.

When someone writes a positive review of your book on Amazon, celebrate. Get yourself an ice cream or a bottle of coke. A glowing review really makes a writer's day. This is why I'm constantly on a lookout for new reviews of my books. Whenever I see that there's a new review, I take the time to read it. The bad reviews that I get on some of my books upset me, but the positive reviews really warm my heart. I really feel blessed when I know that I've touched someone's life and given them a real positive experience from my books.

Celebrate your reviews and make a point of encouraging yourself and being happy. If you find that your books are lacking in reviews, there's a site that I'll mention under one of my videos called InkSpand.com where you can pay a reviewer to do one for you. For only $25 you can ask someone to make a review of your book. $25 per review is for the whole system to operate, but each of the readers get paid $10. I've read a few books there and got paid $10 to read them and I enjoy writing good reviews. I enjoy reading people's books and writing reviews for them.

Tip 29 - Write your next book.

There really is nothing to do, is there? When you've published your book, you have good reviews coming in and you're happy because you've changed some people's lives, the next step is to write your next book. A writer doesn't stop writing just because they've finished one book. Get on the horse, get some inspiration and write your next book.

Before I leave you to it, allow me to give you a little prayer to see you off.

Dear Father,

I pray that you would inspire and be with each of the readers who read this. I pray that you'll inspire them so they'll become a writer. I pray that they can get the right chapter titles for their book. I pray that you be with them, to move with them, to walk with them each step of the way. I pray that you lead them, to keep them inspired, to encourage and help them to write each page of their book up until the last page. I pray that you give them the finances to get the book edited and give them the patience to persist in getting the book published. I pray that one day, when their book is published, that they'll actually write to me at my email address and tell me about their book so I can read it and write a review for them. I pray that you bless them, keep them safe and lead them into every success. In Jesus' name, Amen.

Section 3
11 Tips to getting your book published

In this section, you will find that I have repeated some things that I have already said beforehand in this book. There are two reasons for this. First, the material for Section 2 of the video and the book originally came from this section. This makes Section 2 a repeat of this section, rather than the other way around. Second is that I feel the need to include the repeated information because it is important in getting the point of my tips across. With that said, I pray that these tips will bless you.

TIP 1: Get a title for your book.

First thing's first is that you need to get a title for your book. You may have ideas about what you're going to write or what you want to do with the book. However, everything springs off from the title. For instance, I've written a book that's titled *"The Parables of Jesus Made Simple."* In just that simple title, I've managed to explain the main idea of the book. One is that it's a book about parables, and two is that it's a book that's simple to read. Compared to other books on the parables of Jesus that I've read, mine simplifies the language used, making it highly readable and more accessible. Another book I wrote was called *"His Redeeming Love - A memoir."* From that book you can glean that it's about my life and the overarching theme is that even if you've done bad things in life, Jesus will always be there to redeem you. The book also makes use of this verse: "All things work together for good for those who love God and are called according to his purpose," Romans 8:28. From these examples, you'll understand that you'll want to be able to capture what your book is about in a title. I'm not saying that you should come up with your title straight away, but it's good to have at least a working title. That is a title that you work under before you come up with the final title.

I am not sure if you can hear the Holy Spirit really well, but it'll help if you did. I would like to say that a book title is easy to get when the Holy Spirit gives it to you. I like to think that all of my titles come from the Holy Spirit. The title also needs to have a searchable term or theme so that when people search it on Amazon books, they could easily find it. One of my books is called *"Prophetic Evangelism Made Simple - Prophetic Seed Sowing."* Many people recognize the term "prophetic evangelism" these days and would be searching under those terms. The simplicity of the title tells the person that the book is easier to understand than most. The Prophetic seed sowing part of the title is the one that speaks to the attitude of the person. In time, readers will understand this more as they read the book.

If you're stumped about what your book title should be, ask your friends for some suggestions. For instance, if you're at a loss in choosing which of the two or three titles you've thought you should go for, then ask your friends for a consensus. It's important to realize that your friends are readers and they may have good opinions about your work. They can also provide you with an objective view that you might not have yourself. You need not make the final decision on your title till you get the book cover designed, but it really helps if you have the title while you are writing your book. Keep your title simple, to the point, and give your reader an idea what to expect out of your book. That is how you make a good title.

TIP 2: Write your chapter titles clearly.

How do you go from a title to a whole book? In my case, after I have my title, I put on some anointed music and let the Holy Spirit come to me. Once He starts flowing through me, I get out a writing pad and I write the chapter titles that pop in my head consecutively. From chapter one, I start to build a foundation for the book. I'll build a foundation through chapter one, chapter two, and chapter three. I consecutively make my points and make a title for each chapter.

It's possible for you to work on 20 or 40 chapter titles in just one sitting. Just make sure that they have a natural flow in them. You can change them later on, but it's good to get a list of 20 to 40. In my case I was able to write the chapter titles of most of my books in just under five minutes. Just like the title of the book, the chapter title should perfectly describe what's going to happen in that chapter. Some non-fiction writers have books that have fancy chapter titles that readers won't understand until they've read the chapter. I've never understood the appeal since I've never written a book like that. I like my chapter titles to be plainly understood and become more understood the more people read the chapter. Thus, it is important that you clearly understand from your chapter title what your chapter is going to be about.

TIP 3: Put on some good Christian music.

My third tip is something that is applicable only if you happen to write Christian books like me. When I sit down to write, I usually pick up some "Jesus Culture," "Misty Edwards" or some sort of worship music on my iTunes. I find that anointed music really sets the atmosphere and allows my creative juices to start flowing. It also brings me into an anointed state where the Holy Spirit can speak through me. I like to think that the Holy Spirit is a co-writer of mine and, in the right moments, takes hold of me as I write.

By using anointed music, I allow my thoughts to flow through my mind and into the page. I don't stop typing, I don't stop at any stage to think, and I don't pause. When I sit down, I usually write two A4 pages in one sitting. That takes about a whole album or two to play while I write.

TIP 4: Write two to four pages on each chapter.

Whatever you choose, whether it's to write two A4 pages or four, make sure it's consistent. You can say something in two pages that can be quite comprehensive, maybe even make a good argument in it. Please be aware, however, that you always have the next chapter to add on to what you're saying. That's why it's important to write your chapter titles to consecutively and progressively impart information. They're the building blocks at the beginning of your book, a foundation for what you're going to say later. Whether you choose to write two A4 pages or four A4 pages, keep it consistent.

It is important to write the same amount in each chapter consistently, so that a reader can be confident of the length of each chapter. As a reader, you'll probably be confused if one chapter was four pages, and the next chapter was six pages. Like I have said before, if you are going to write more than your average chapter length, try and split it into two chapters instead.

TIP 5: When you've written your whole book, go through it slowly, chapter by chapter.

When you have finished writing your book, make sure to go over it again slowly. As I said before, I usually go through each of my chapters and proofread them a little bit once I finish them. There's a chance that by reading your book again, you might be able to add more content to certain chapters. Giving your book another read gives you an overall understanding of your whole book. It lets you see whether you need to add anything or change anything in the book. It also gives you the opportunity to proofread and change any grammatical errors that you may have missed.

TIP 6: Hire a copy editor.

Again, I want to stress the importance of hiring a copy editor to polish your work. A copy editor is someone who takes your writing and transforms it into something really good. They can take your sentences and turn them into something readable. Once they're done with the work, they can send you a copy of all the changes they've made. I don't usually request that, but I do know that if you make the request they can send it in Microsoft Word format and show you all the changes they've made. I personally don't like the editing process so I don't look at those things. I just re-read what they have to say and change it or keep it as is. They're the experts.

Now the copy editor may rewrite things but there's always a chance that they can make errors in your work. They are not infallible. So it makes good sense to have another set of eyes to go over your work as a proofreader.

Once you had a copy editor go through your work, hire a proofreader to go through it to see if the copy editor made any errors. Then after that, it's advisable to go through your work one last time to see if the proofreader himself missed anything. One of the hardest things to do in a book is to get all the errors out. If you think you're used to seeing books with typos and all sorts of things, think again. Most self-published books come with a lot of typos, and that's because not every self-publisher has the means to proofread them. For instance, Create Space, one of the best self-publishing firms owned by Amazon, doesn't proofread your book for you. They'll publish a book with errors in it and they won't even know because they'll just publish it without reading it. It's up to you to get all the errors out. That's why hiring a copy editor and getting yourself a proofreader are equally important.

I stress the need for this because it's important to get the errors out of your book. When a work is riddled with typographical and grammatical errors, expect readers to retaliate with one negative review after another. Nothing is more painful than reading a negative review that says, "It was a good book in content, but he needs better editors." I've learned from my mistakes and I do my best to get errors out of my books.

TIP 7: Review your book yourself.

Once you have written your book and had a copy editor rewrite and polish it, take the time to read it again. When you reread it, make sure the editor has rewritten your book to say exactly what you want said. Sometimes, they might not understand something that you've written and have rewritten something that is different than what you meant. Once you have done a run through and fixed everything that needs to be fixed, get a proofreader to go through your book again. Once they're done with their work, make sure that you reread your book one more time before you give it to your publisher. I cannot stress that last part enough. Errors in your book can really hurt book sales, especially if people say that in a review. The problem about Amazon is that it is a community that relies on honest reviews, so even negative reviews on your book cannot be taken down by you. If you want to save time and money and think that your book has no errors in it, it's a risk that you have to take on your own.

TIP 8: Have an experienced writer write the back cover.

Have an experienced writer write the back cover blurb for your book. Usually I give the honors to my copy editor, who has read the book countless times while editing it. She's written blurbs for three of my books now. I have a deal with her that she'll write the blurb if I mention her name as the editor on Amazon when I publish the book. This allows her to get more work and adds to her portfolio. She does my blurbs for free simply because I advertise her name on Amazon.

I would advise against writing a blurb for your own book yourself. An experienced writer will be able to read your book and distill it into a creative description on the back cover. The trouble with doing it on your own is that your intimate involvement in the book's creation prevents you from writing about it objectively.

I learned of this from another person's book about how to create a successful book on Kindle. The book also talked about the five most important things to make your book a success.

1. Good content. It's up to you to make sure your book has the very best content that it can have.

2. It is vital that your book has been edited and proof read to make sure it is error free.

3. It is vital that your book has a compelling blurb

4. It is very important that your book has a cover that stands out.

5. Your book's success depends on how many positive reviews it has on Amazon.

TIP 9: Get yourself a publisher.

Create Space does a very good job in helping self-publishers get their work off the ground. Of all the self-publishing firms on the market, Create Space offers the best service. I currently use another little Christian publisher that does a great personal service on my books. One good thing about Create Space is that they can let you make as little on your book as you like. For many years, I always thought that the cheaper I made my paperback books, the more people would buy them. Other self-publishing firms don't allow you to set a minimal amount for your book like Create Space does.

As a Christian author who has published five books with Create Space, I thought I had found the best publisher for me. Yet, I still managed to find a smaller publisher, Revival Waves and Glory Publishing, which does a more comprehensive job of publishing my books. Not only do they prepare your manuscript and print your paperbacks, but they also arrange for your books to be converted to all eBook formats and distribute them to over a thousand eBook retailers. Bill Vincent, the person who runs the publishing firm, also gives you a wide range of good advertising plans that you can choose from. These plans help advertise your book to Christian bookstores and will stock them when they order your book. The plans also include making an audio book from your book which they can sell on Audible, the biggest audio book retailer owned by Amazon. I don't even consider producing my books through Create Space anymore since Bill has proven to be a personal friend. For those who want to make use of his services, I have his website address at the end of the book in the resources section.

Here's something interesting that I want to share. When I was starting out, I couldn't publish my books on Apple iTunes since it requires me to have an American bank account and tax number. I also couldn't use the Audio book making company that Amazon suggested because I was not an American Citizen. With Bill acting as my publisher however, these hurdles have been overcome and the books I have published through Revival Waves and Glory

Publishing are now available through iTunes. They are also in the process of making them into audio books, so if you happen to be someone living outside the USA and you want to get a hold of my works, you might find this information very interesting.

TIP 10: Hire a graphic designer for the cover.

Presentation is key. Having an unprofessional cover is always detrimental to your book sales. You can have great material in it, have it well-edited and proofread, but if your book cover isn't pleasing, it just won't sell. People really do judge a book by its cover. Just go through Amazon and look at the books. Chances are, you can quickly sort out the self-published books from the corporate-published book because the former has covers that are just not good.

You can hire a Freelance graphic designer to do your cover. When hiring your graphic designer, ask them if they could show you some covers that they have produced in the past. If they want to win the bid to do the job, they will show you what they are capable of. I have a designer who has done good book covers for me and I've also listed her name in the resources section at the end of this book. I am sure she will be happy to make a cover for you.

Many times, I had a good idea of what I wanted to have on my cover. It'll be a big help to you and your designer if you are able to visualize it down to the smallest detail. But if not, I'm sure that a competent graphic designer can create a good cover for you if you can just explain what your book is all about.

A good cover is essential to the success of your book, so make sure you don't try to do it on your own if you don't have the skills to do it or have some inferior cover designed by an incompetent graphic designer. I learned this from publishing my unsuccessful book, The Musings of a Mad Prophet. Not only did the book have an unclear theme and didn't have an attractive title, but it also did not have a picture on its cover. All of these elements contributed to the book's unpopularity, and it ended up not selling many copies over the years.

You don't have to accept a cover unless it is a good one. In my case, I use a Filipino designer so my covers only cost me $60. This is cheaper compared to the $600 that a Western designer can charge you. I believe in spending money to make sure my books end up having the best quality it deserves, but I simply can't afford to throw good money away on a Western designer.

You cannot have the final edition of the cover designed until the graphic designer knows how many pages your book has. You will need Create Space or Bill to produce the internal PDF for your book before you have the designer produce your cover. Once you are happy with the cover, you can finally send it in PDF format to your publisher.

TIP 11: You need to get reviews.

As I have mentioned before in this book, you will need good reviews for your book to be a success. If your book doesn't have favorable reviews, people wouldn't read it, even if it was offered to them for free. One of the best reasons I shop on Amazon is that I like to read the reviews. I actually place more stock in a couple of top voted reviews on a book than I do on the publisher's blurb of the book. Anyone with skill can write a blurb for a book, but most of the time, it's the reviews that are written by readers that will point you in the right direction.

Many times I have read a couple of bad reviews for a book and have taken the reviewer's opinion seriously. It saved me from purchasing books that may prove to be a waste of time and money in the end.

In my experience, I've found that people who don't know you too well will respect you more and read your book and write reviews for you. But while those people are a more apt choice when it comes to looking for an objective review, approaching your friends to ask them the same is still a viable solution. I have had a few personal friends write reviews for me on Amazon, but most of my reviews have come from friends on Facebook.

Just today, I have come across a person who can read your book and can write a comprehensive review for you. She can't publish it on Amazon yet, but you can freely publish it on your book page under Editorial Reviews. This will have a good effect on your book sales.

If you're in need of reviews, there's also Inkspand.com, the website I have mentioned before, who have readers that can write you a review for a modest fee. Both of these reviewers will be mentioned in my resources page at the end of this book.

Final Words

I read a book once about how to write good books. The writer of that book bluntly said that if you happen to be reading his book, chances are you're just delaying the process of sitting down and writing your own book. He suggested that you put his book down, go and write your book, and then come back only when the book is finished and you want to edit it into a better book. I did not start this book with that intention. I personally believe that the information that I have given you in this book can be very helpful information to a new writer.

As a writer who has self-published eight books and who has another four in the process of being prepared for publishing, I felt that I had learned some good tips that I wanted to share. I didn't plan on sharing this information just for the sake of writing another book. I wrote the book to help readers who want to become writers one day. I went to the expense of time and money to record the videos, pay for them to be transcribed, rewrite and edit the book, and have the book copy edited to produce a good message that will be helpful.

I don't think any book should be written just for the sake of writing a book. As I edited this book, I realized that this is the kind of book that I wished I could have found when I first attempted to publish my own work for the first time. As you go through the steps on how to write your book and publish it, things will get tough and sometimes, you might think you cannot go on. But press on and try to persevere.

There are some things in this book you will find that I didn't talk about in detail. For instance, I haven't included every step you need to do to create a Create Space book. This book also doesn't provide answers to the questions you might ask Bill Vincent my publisher. There are books or videos that can explain the process to take with publishing via Create Space and I have not included that information in this book.

Again, ask yourself these questions before you write: Do I have a message that is going to impact lives for the glory of God? Do I have something to say that will help people if they read it and understand it? Do I have the desire to spend as much money and time as it takes to influence these people that will read my book? If your answers are yes, then you might want to ask God for the inspiration to write your first book.

May God bless you with your writing!

Matthew Robert Payne

July 2015

Resources mentioned in this book.

Create Space can be found at
https://www.createspace.com

At the time, Create Space was the most professional self-publishing platform that I had found while researching for a publisher for my books. Since finding Bill Vincent though, I opted not to use their services again unless Bill went out of business in the publishing industry.

Revival Waves of Glory Publishing - Bill Vincent can be found at

http://www.revivalwavesofgloryministries.com/publishing.html

This is the best publisher that I have found and use to date. Thanks to this publisher, I now have my books in Christian bookstores, which was something that I couldn't achieve back when I was using Create Space. Bill has a wide range of attractive publishing packages and goes above and beyond the course of duty. He adds a personal touch to his work. Bill prayerfully considers all his potential clients.

Upwork - A website for freelance workers that can be found at

https://www.upwork.com

Here you can hire someone to transcribe, copy edit, proofread, and write professional blurbs for your books. You can also hire someone to create a website for you.

Maria Quiocho - My Graphic designer

Maria can be found and hired on Upwork.com. She is a very competent graphic designer and I use her for most of my books. She would be happy to work for you.

Melanie Cardano - My Copy Editor

Melanie is a competent Copy Editor who does a very good job with my books. She also writes my blurbs for me. She can be hired on Upork.com.

Inkspand - Book reviews can be found at
https://www.inkspand.com

For $25, you can get this website to make a review for your work. If you happen to be a reviewer looking for work, the cut is $10 for every review that you write. If you like the review, the reviewer can post it on Amazon and Barnes and Noble for you.

Kathy's Notes Book Reviews can be found at:
http://www.kathysnotes.com/blog/paid-book-reviews-honest-reviews-only-no-spoilers

Kathy can write a review between 250 words and 700 words that can be published on your Amazon book page under the section "Editorial Reviews." Kathy will publish her review for you on Goodreads, a popular book promotion site.

I'd love to hear from you.

One easy way to let me know what you think of this book is to post an honest review on Amazon for me. Many people, including me, don't make a decision to buy a book until they have read a few reviews on Amazon. If you enjoyed this book and it was helpful to you, you can really be a blessing to me and write a review for me. It is easy, it is simple, and it might just help a person decide to buy this book and then go on and write a powerful well read book!

You can contact me:

I would love to hear from you. If you want to share a book that you're going to write and you want me to read and review it in the future, please feel free to contact me at any of these places below.

My website at http://matthewrobertpayneministries.net/

For a prophecy off me see http://personal-prophecy-today.com

At this prophetic website there is also a donation page that you can sow money into my book writing ministry.

My email at survivors.sanctuary@gmail.com

My Facebook Group I administer at https://www.facebook.com/groups/OpenHeavensGroup/

Other books by Matthew Robert Payne

The Parables of Jesus Made Simple.

The Prophetic Supernatural Experience

Prophetic Evangelism Made Simple

Kingdom Nuggets- A Handbook for Christian Living

Your Identity in Christ.

His Redeeming Love- A Memoir

Great Cloud of Witnesses Speak